The
WELFARE
STATE

For
Amelia and Rebecca

To Lindsay Frost with best wishes from the Author DFraser 4/02

SUTTON POCKET HISTORIES

THE
WELFARE
STATE

DEREK FRASER

SUTTON PUBLISHING

First published in 2000 by
Sutton Publishing Limited · Phoenix Mill
Thrupp · Stroud · Gloucestershire · GL5 2BU

British Library Cataloguing in Publication Data
A catalogue record for this book is available from the British
Library.

ISBN 0-7509-2290-7

Cover picture: A detail from a cartoon by George Whitelaw
showing Beveridge fighting the five giants: want, ignorance,
disease, squalor, idleness.

Typeset in 11/14.5 pt Baskerville.
Typesetting and origination by
Sutton Publishing Limited.
Printed and bound in England by
J.H. Haynes & Co. Ltd, Sparkford.

Contents

Acknowledgements

I am grateful to the series editor, my dear friend and mentor, Asa Briggs, for persuading me to write this volume and thereby forcing me to rekindle my historical interest in the Welfare State.

I am much indebted to the historians and social scientists whose recent scholarship has greatly enlarged my understanding of the contemporary welfare system and its historical antecedents. I owe a particular debt of gratitude to Alan Deacon, both for bibliographic advice and for his kindness in agreeing to review my manuscript. Margaret Gibson produced the text with her characteristic efficiency and good humour. I thank her as a friend and colleague.

List of Dates

1942	Beveridge Report
1943	*Education Reconstruction* White Paper
1944	White Papers *Social Insurance, Employment Policy, A National Health Service*; Beveridge, *Full Employment in a Free Society*; Education Act
1945	Family Allowances Act; Labour landslide – Attlee PM
1946	National Insurance Act; National Insurance (Industrial Injuries) Act; National Health Service Act
1948	National Assistance Act
5 July 1948	Appointed Day – Welfare State created
1951	Churchill PM
1959	Macmillan 'Never had it so good' election
1966	Supplementary Benefits; Ministry of Social Security
1975	Social Security Acts
1976	IMF crisis
1979	Margaret Thatcher PM
1985–86	Fowler Review
1990	National Health Service and Community Care Act
1997	Labour victory – Blair PM
1998–2000	Welfare to Work; New Deal; Green Paper *A New Contract for Welfare*

ONE

Introduction: Definitions and Perspectives

The Welfare State is indelibly bound up with the historical experience of the British people during the 1940s. In 1948, the Labour government created a 'cradle to grave' welfare system, based upon the famous Beveridge Report of 1942. Definitions of the Welfare State are closely entwined with the British experience. Thus the 1998 *New Oxford Dictionary* defines a welfare state as

> A system whereby the state undertakes to protect the health
> and well-being of its citizens, especially those in financial or
> social need, by means of grants, pensions and other benefits.
> The foundations for the modern welfare state in the UK
> were laid by the Beveridge Report of 1942.

This close association is confirmed in the *Encyclopaedia Britannica* entry which explains that 'The

1

modern use of the term is associated with the comprehensive measures of social insurance adopted in 1948 by Great Britain on the basis of the Beveridge Report.'

The Beveridge-inspired Welfare State was the boon which Britain conferred on western society after the Second World War. As Beveridge himself told the future Prime Minister, Harold Wilson, 'From now on, Beveridge is not the name of a man: it is the name of a way of life, and not only for Britain, but for the whole civilised world.' The Welfare State so clearly defined in both time and character is the subject of this book, which seeks to explain its origins and development and its first half-century of history. In summary terms, the outline history is clear.

An understanding of the British Welfare State must begin with the Victorian Poor Law. This is because the whole history of welfare policy in the twentieth century may be viewed as a reaction to, and contradiction of, the harsh values and social stigma associated with the Poor Law. Paradoxically, many services which grew up under the aegis of the Poor Law were later incorporated into what later became the Welfare State. A key turning-point may be identified in the Liberal governments before the First World War, which introduced the principle of statutory social insurance to the British people. The exigencies of war in the 1940s completed the process and led to the creation of the Welfare State in 1948.

Beneath that simple chronology lay complex political, social and economic forces which suggest a pluralistic historical explanation for the rise of the Welfare State. In the first flush of enthusiasm for the Welfare State, many historians understandably saw the history of British social policy as essentially a triumph of progressive ideas. Benevolent and well-intentioned reformers identified social evils to be addressed by a state agenda and radical thinkers developed ideologies to restrain and correct the workings of industrial capitalism. Yet these were never value-free interventions and, often, social policy was inspired by ideas of social engineering or social control. There were behavioural objectives in much social policy, which sometimes took on the character of a cultural assault by the privileged upon the mores of the disadvantaged. At other times the behavioural social-control stick was the price to be paid for the welfare benefit carrot.

Social policy was also closely associated with the development of an administrative infrastructure which could translate ideology into practical policy solutions. Beveridge himself and his most similar forerunner, Edwin Chadwick, were both essentially bureaucrats, and it was often officials rather than politicians who both inspired and implemented change. Welfare policy in Britain clearly was also bound up with the growing democracy of the British parliamentary system, and welfare policy often had strong electoral motivations. It should also be said that the growth of more radical ideas associated with social democracy could inspire fear of revolutionary change. As a result social reform was sometimes seen as an antidote to socialism. This was quite explicit in the social insurance policy introduced by Bismarck to Germany in the 1880s.

The historical legacy of welfare was thus no simple linear and inevitable progress towards the Welfare State. Contingency was always important. The more, then, that historians study specific social policy initiatives and innovations, the more they find incremental, pragmatic responses to pressing social and political imperatives. Rarely did policy-makers foresee the full implications and consequences of their actions, and social policy often had to deal with the unintended consequences of the previous stage of development. If the Welfare State was itself the product of a complex evolutionary process, the experience of the Welfare State in practice was to complicate the picture even further. Partly this was due to the maturing of the Welfare State as it entered its second quarter-century of existence, and partly to a growing interest in comparative welfare provision in an international context.

When the Welfare State began, it appeared to the British people to be something very special and unique; and such a conclusion was reinforced as overseas visitors came to the United Kingdom to have free operations on the NHS and by the first wave of package-tour travellers who saw, at first hand, in the 1950s and 1960s the shortcomings of welfare provision abroad.

This popular perception soon had to be modified by two strands in analytical thinking about welfare systems. First, it became apparent that countries which were overtly *not* welfare states and which largely eschewed state action, might, nevertheless, achieve better welfare outputs than in Britain. For example, much attention has been focused on the percentage of GDP spent in particular societies on health care. The rhetoric and public debate about health care in Britain has always been about the excessive and spiralling cost of the National Health Service. Yet it turns out that on a comparative international scale British expenditure on the National Health Service is actually less. By the 1990s it was revealed that Britain spent half as much percentage of GDP on health care than did the USA and significantly less than France or Germany. This was brought into sharp focus by the March 2000 budget which allocated significantly increased resources for the NHS, but which would need to be sustained for four years in succession merely to reach the average of European Community expenditure. This and other evidence led to a growing understanding that there were many ways to deal with the social conditions which lay at the heart of the British Welfare State. The British way now became but one of the possible methods of addressing fundamental social and political problems.

The second strand, clearly related to the first, was that there were several types of welfare state and not simply one. Indeed, it became increasingly common to argue that welfare states were associated with an advanced stage of western capitalism and, therefore, were characteristic of the process of modernisation. Rather than seeing the British Welfare State as the ideal type, which then spread its influence around the world, social scientists are now able to categorise a typology of welfare states. One such describes 'Three Worlds of Welfare', a corporatist–conservative model, a liberal–market model and a social-democratic model. The corporatist–conservative model might be found in the state-driven, insurance-based systems of central Europe, which provide high benefits, but few universal services. The liberal-market model with a minimalist approach would best sum up the USA, with some state responsibility for a minimum and the market responsible for anything else. The social-democratic model, usually associated with Sweden, provides an extensive range of services and covers individuals for a wide range of earnings-related benefits. Not all variants would be encompassed within this typology which excludes the paternalistic company welfare systems of Japan or South Korea and the family responsibility system characteristic of China.

It is not at all obvious into which category one would place the British Welfare State. It is an indication of changed perceptions that probably in 1948 the British Welfare State would be character-ised as socialistic and social-democratic, but that by the end of the twentieth century Britain appeared nearer to the USA in providing only a minimum standard. As we shall find, the very development of the Welfare State in Britain changed its essential character and caused social scientists to rethink their definitions. As the phrase now has it, the Welfare State is a much more contested concept than it was at its birth. While the history of social policy is predominantly concerned with the growing responsibility of the state (and this book conforms largely to that pattern), in fact, modern welfare systems are partnerships between the state, the individual, the family, community voluntary provi-sion and employers. We now talk about a 'mixed economy' of welfare, and the task for the historian is to explain why, in a given set of social and historical circumstances, the particular mix of welfare providers is generated. So if we take the example of voluntary charitable provision, this appears at certain periods to be a defence against state intervention and a representation of an altern-ative value system, while at other times it is a supplement to state provision and, indeed, in modern welfare systems often an agent of the state, which has generated the so-called Third Sector in modern Britain. Indeed this sector would have a role to play in Giddens' 'Third Way', which has inspired the Blair government to find a middle way between socialism and capitalism and to adapt social welfare to the realities of globalism.

The modern complexity of welfare systems is further exemplified in the competing ideologies and value systems which now co-exist. One of the essential characteristics of the Beveridge-based Welfare State was the unconditional nature of the citizenship approach to social insurance. There was no need for moralistic judgment about character when social welfare benefits depended upon contractual entitlement earned by insurance con- tributions. It was, to paraphrase Winston Churchill, to take the morality out and put the mathematics in. Yet the essentially altruistic approach to a citizens' Welfare State led some to question whether this did not produce a moral nihilism, in which there were no behavioural objectives and no moral conclusions drawn about consequences. If, as some were arguing by the 1980s, the consequence of the Welfare State was demoralisation, dependency and fraud, then surely some action was needed to put moralism back into the equation.

If the poor and disadvantaged were not to be treated simply as victims, then their desire for self-action and self-improvement would have to be rekindled. From Jeremy Bentham in the early nineteenth century to Beveridge in the mid-twentieth century, and to the American political scientist, Charles Murray, there has been a belief in the freedom of choice of the rational economic person making decisions on the basis of personal advantage. It has therefore been argued, at the end of the twentieth century, that the Welfare State needs to re-institute incentives that will conduce to the individual and collective good. Of course, there are dangers that if individuals pursue their own self-interests and that takes them outside the mutuality of the Welfare State, then society is the poorer. As the sociologist Bauman has explained it, 'the process leads inevitably to relentless deterioration of collective services . . . which prompts those who can to buy themselves out from collective provision – an act which turns out to mean, sooner or later, buying themselves out of collective responsibility.'

The balance between individualism and collectivism, between state provision and voluntary provision, between the self-acting actuarialism of insurance and the behavioural imperatives of moralism and between universalism and selectivity, lie at the heart of the debate about the nature, character and future of the British Welfare State in the twenty-first century. These debates have their historical antecedents and to place them in a historical context is vital to an understanding of the dynamics of the British Welfare State.

TWO

The Victorian Origins of the Welfare State

There was no Welfare State in Victorian England. The values and philosophy, the objectives and benevolence of a welfare state, together with the aspirations and expectations promoted by a welfare state are indelibly connected to the twentieth century. As the *Financial Times* put it in a retrospective editorial at the end of the millennium, 'From Bismarck to Beveridge to Franklin D. Roosevelt and beyond, the 20th century was the century of the Welfare State'. It is therefore an anachronism to talk about a Victorian welfare state even in embryo.

However, there were elements of state welfare in Victorian England. The central plank was the famous new Poor Law, the creation of the Poor Law Amendment Act of 1834, described recently by

Englander as 'the single most important piece of social legislation ever enacted'. As the title of the legislation indicates, the Victorian Poor Law was an adaptation and a reform of the old Poor Law which dates back to the Tudors. Collated together at the end of the Tudor reign, the so-called 43rd of Elizabeth placed a legal obligation upon parishes to relieve destitution. Over the next two centuries the Poor Law proved to be a very flexible and adaptable social instrument, responding in a local context to changing circumstances.

The Poor Law faced its greatest challenge when the combination of industrial revolution, agrarian revolution and the Napoleonic wars combined together at the end of the eighteenth century and the beginning of the nineteenth century to place enormous pressure upon the social fabric. Economic and social dislocation, rising prices and increased unemployment called for some extreme measures. The Poor Law responded by increasing Poor Law allowances in order to prevent starvation. The consequence was that the cost of poor relief quad-rupled between 1790 and 1820. The soaring cost of relief, together with continued social discontent manifested in both urban and rural disorder, greatly worried contemporaries who were uneasy and fearful about what was happening to economy and society. Moreover, informed public opinion was beginning to absorb a new ideology that accompanied the rise of industrial capitalism.

From Adam Smith's *Wealth of Nations* they learned the value of the free market and free competition in what became known as the *laissez-faire* philosophy. The seven editions of *Principles of Population* by Thomas Malthus taught that population growth would outstrip the economy's capacity to absorb it and that allowances for children (as widely dispensed within the old Poor Law), were placing a premium upon child birth which was wholly counter-productive. This was reinforced by David Ricardo's theory of the wage fund, which suggested that the more taken out of the fund in poor relief, the less would be available in wages. The 'dismal' science of political economy was mediated for the early nineteenth century through the utilitarianism of Jeremy Bentham, with his greatest happiness principle. Institutions were to be judged as to whether they had conduced to the greatest happiness of the greatest number and were to be subjected to the strict test of efficiency and

14

effectiveness. It was two key disciples of Jeremy Bentham, an academic economist Nassau Senior and the archetypal bureaucrat Edwin Chadwick, who were effectively the authors of the Poor Law Amendment Act of 1834.

In 1832 Parliament set up a Royal Commission to inquire into the supposed evils of the old Poor Law and to make recommendations for its reform. Historians have been much kinder to the old Poor Law in the last half-century of its existence than was the Royal Commission. It is now felt that the alleged excesses of the old Poor Law were rational and not unreasonable responses to an economic and social crisis. This opinion found little echo in the report of the Royal Commission. Though the largest ever inquiry and evidence-gathering exercise and though, theoretically, the empirical basis for subsequent legislation, it was in fact used by Senior and Chadwick to justify preconceived views. The central criticism was that the allowance system in aid of wages had altered the natural balance of individual welfare. Inspired by both the invisible hand of Adam Smith and the utilitarianism of Jeremy Bentham, Chadwick's report argued that the dice had been loaded in favour of indolence rather than industry.

Expressing an idea that echoes over the ages, the 1834 Poor Law report condemned those recent developments which had made it more beneficial for the individual to be out of work rather than in it.

The solution appeared to be deceptively simple. If policy could reverse the conditions, such that independent work and labour yielded a standard of living perceptibly higher than that which could be achieved on public welfare, then individuals would have the strongest inducement to leave the pauper class and join the labouring class. This was the famous principle of 'less eligibility', where the level of relief would always be depressed below that which an able-bodied adult male could acquire for himself. In order to reinforce and exemplify this less eligible standard of welfare, the 1834 report advocated the workhouse test, for which the new Poor Law was to become infamous. In place of the unscientific allocations of doles, whether in money or kind, would be appropriately managed relief in well-regulated workhouses, where the different categories of pauper could be treated in a manner relevant to their conditions. As a true Benthamite, Chadwick advocated strong centralisation and uniformity and suggested that the 15,000 parishes,

16

with their multifarious local practices, should be collapsed into some 600 poor law unions supervised by a centralised authority.

The Poor Law report, which took two years to complete and contained a mass of valuable local and national research, was used as a spurious justification for the legislation which followed. Though condemned by historians as being both wildly unhistorical and wildly unstatistical, the Poor Law report was within several months enacted as the Poor Law Amendment Act. A central Poor Law Commission was established with Chadwick as its secretary, and the new Poor Law was introduced into England and Wales with the key characteristics of less eligibility, the workhouse test, and administrative centralisation and uniformity. The clear aim was to reduce the cost of poor relief, to ensure greater efficiency in administration, to encourage individual effort and to significantly reduce outdoor relief in favour of appropriately designed indoor relief. The most important central aim of the new Poor Law as created in 1834 was to deter pauperism and not to solve the problem of poverty. The distinction between pauperism, by which was meant destitution, and poverty, by which was understood the condition of the majority of the population who had recourse only to their own labour, is fundamental to an understanding of the Victorian welfare system.

The new Poor Law was introduced and parishes were united into unions; workhouses were built and attempts were made to restrict outdoor relief for able-bodied adult males. The introduction of the new Poor Law into the industrial Midlands and North coincided with a trade depression, which revealed all too clearly the inappropriateness of the workhouse system to deal with mass unemployment. There were serious riots in the industrial North in 1837 and 1838, resisting the new Poor Law and creating that climate of hatred and fear of the Bastilles, as the workhouses soon became known, which has transcended the generations ever since. When the new Poor Law was introduced into those recalcitrant areas, it was necessary to tone down the full rigour of the workhouse test and in practice outdoor relief continued. This was fuelled by both common sense and economy. It was soon apparent that it was far cheaper to relieve people within their own homes by a paltry dole than to give them full subsistence within an institution. A desire to keep poor rates down, which is a common wish of all taxpayers in all generations, combined with the impracticality of taking very large numbers of paupers and their families into the workhouse, meant that the centralised and uniform system dreamed of by Chadwick never materialised in full implementation.

However, over time the new Poor Law did settle down and the number of paupers in receipt of relief did fall steadily through the Victorian period. The overall number of paupers receiving relief in England and Wales fell from one and a quarter million in 1834 (8.8 per cent of the population), to 800,000 in 1880, by then some 3 per cent of the population. In a sense the aim of the 1834 Poor Law reforms, to deter pauperism and reduce Poor Law expenditure, was indeed fulfilled in the first half-century of its existence. It is equally true that, over time, the number of adult able-bodied male paupers did reduce, though it may be that local poor law unions used their discretion to support some adult males under the flexible catch-all category of 'sudden and urgent necessity', as well as sickness, incapacity or old age.

In general, unions found themselves dealing with twice as many females as males, who were grouped in categories for which the test of both less eligibility and the workhouse were wholly inappropriate. Widows, deserted wives, unmarried mothers, aged and infirm spinsters had of necessity frequent recourse to the Poor Law, although they figured little in the report or the thinking of the day. The same was true of the elderly, whose need was hardly the result of personal failing in a society where even those in regular work could hardly make adequate provision for their old age. The sick were also in need of temporary care and support rather than permanent incarceration within a workhouse. The predominance of short-term unemployment or under-employment, gender-related distress, sickness, old age, and incapacity and family breakdown all tended to suggest remedies that would often be better directed outside the workhouse than within it. Hence the proportion of paupers receiving indoor relief did not dramatically increase in the first decades of the new Poor Law. At least until the third quarter of the nineteenth century only one in approximately six paupers was relieved inside the workhouse. From the 1870s when there was renewed assault on outdoor relief, the proportion of paupers did increase, so that by the end of the century around 25 to 30 per cent of all paupers were now receiving indoor relief. It has been estimated that perhaps 80 per cent of all those who experienced indoor relief within the workhouse were there as emergency urgent cases, and left the workhouse after a short period.

Part of the intentional deterrent effect of the workhouse was that the regime within should be disciplined and harsh and clearly only acceptable to those who were in genuinely dire need. Workhouse regimes were part of the way in which the central Poor Law Commission (replaced by a Poor Law Board in 1847 and by the Local Government Board in 1871) enforced its centralisation and administrative uniformity. The central authority and its inspectors who toured the land advised local unions on the designs of their workhouses, the diets to be provided, the regulations under which appointments were made: the endless bureaucratic requirements of form-filling and statistics required by the central authority were all part of a new administrative imperative which was lacking in previous generations. Of course, while the Poor Law remained locally funded, as it was throughout the nineteenth century and while policy was enacted by elected guardians, there would always be a good deal of local discretion, notwithstanding the image and formality of central control.

We know from the fiction of Dickens as well as the popular folk culture that workhouses were hated institutions. Whether what actually went on in workhouses justified the popular image of cruelty and harshness has been somewhat more problematic in determining. Sadly, we know from our own experience within the welfare state that institutional care for the vulnerable and defenceless can provide opportunities for psychological and even, sometimes, physical abuse. There were undoubtedly scandals in the Victorian Poor Law, and they were often exposed by the very centralised procedure of monitoring and inspection which was characteristic of the system. However, the distaste for the workhouse regimes within the Poor Law were as much about the loss of individual identity as about physical cruelty. On entry to the workhouse individuals were classified and sent to different wards; men, women and children being separated even from within the same family, compulsory dress, workhouse uniform, was enforced, a boring and monotonous daily regime was punctuated by often pointless task work and there was a lack of leisure activity. It was the social control characteristic of all institutions that was resented and generated a healthy fear and distaste for the workhouse. On the other hand, in a paradoxical way the workhouse provided for its inmates a basic diet, sanitary conditions and enforced personal cleanliness, clean clothing, medical care and protection from the elements. Not all of these were readily available to large numbers of those who struggled on outside the workhouse.

It was under the influence of the central authority, though by no means at the pace Chadwick would have wished, that Poor Law officials came to attempt a classification of paupers in order to ensure that they received the treatment appropriate to their reasons for being in the workhouse or on dole relief. Children were a particular case in point. In the mid-nineteenth century some 40 per cent of all paupers were children. Even if they were deemed to be the product of intemperate and feckless behaviour, they were hardly deserving of the harsh treatment and deterrence that characterised the Poor Law generally. Indeed if they were as adults not to be a continuing burden upon society, then it was important that they received at least a basic education. From the earliest days of the new Poor Law there was stress upon providing appropriate schooling for pauper children, either in the 'barrack schools', or within a section of the work-house itself. Generations of pauper children gained a basic education, which again was not widely available to children of the labouring poor.

The same was increasingly true of those who looked to the Poor Law for relief during periods of illness or incapacity. The bureaucratic requirement for information, classification and statistics soon revealed that large numbers of paupers were applying for help because of sickness alone. It therefore became common for such people, par-ticularly families, women and the elderly, to receive assistance for medical treatment and for pharma-ceutical provision. Workhouses contained separate sick wards and these, over time, transformed themselves into dispensaries and hospitals, often in the larger unions in a totally separate building. In some of our great cities the present-day hospitals were built around an original workhouse hospital on the same site. Over time, the discrimination against the sick poor gradually diminished and by

1885 those who applied for poor relief solely for medical help were allowed to retain the right to vote. It was developments such as these which led a number of historians to see in the Poor Law medical services of the mid-nineteenth century the origins of the National Health Service of the twentieth century. A similar story applied in the area of mental health, with the various Lunacy Acts for the provision of separate wards or hospitals for the mentally ill, and referrals to those asylums increased quite significantly during the Victorian period.

By the 1890s it was increasingly common for the stigma of poor relief to be exempted for the elderly. Indeed, in the last quarter of the nineteenth century the Victorian Poor Law adopted a much more specialised approach to the treatment of the poor and became a specialised agency running orphanages, old-age homes, hospitals and dispensaries in a quite varied social service for a limited population. By that period adult male and female paupers were becoming almost non-existent and were forced to rely on other provision. The Poor Law clientele comprised children, the infirm, the disabled and the elderly.

The Goschen Minute of 1869 had a profound effect upon both Poor Law practice and the organisation of philanthropy in the late-Victorian period. It was in order to give greater system and direction to the rich flowering of philanthropy that London reformers came together to form the Charity Organisation Society in 1869. The COS was imbued with the philosophy of self-help and individualism and wished to use charity in order to target assistance to the deserving and to build character. This required knowledge of the individual in need, and the COS was to develop what came to be modern social casework. A combination of scientific analysis, *noblesse oblige*, a good deal of socially superior paternalism and a genuine compassion produced a complex mixture which not all recipients found attractive. COS leaders, including C.S. Loch and Helen Bosanquet, had a major influence on policy-making in late Victorian and Edwardian England. The influence of the COS spread back into the Poor Law itself as relieving officers also came to look into the individual circumstances of paupers and to establish the character and worth of the individual applicant.

28

To extol the virtues of individual responsibility, and to use charitable effort in order to restore self-reliance in those that were temporarily in distress, was to conform to the grain of social thinking which characterised much mid-Victorian opinion. For many the great bible was Samuel Smiles, and his book *Self Help*, which found a ready audience particularly among skilled workers in regular employment. Though the late 1880s were to be characterised as a period of the 'Great Depression', the general trend was for working-class incomes to rise because of falling prices. With disposable income came attention to longer-term needs, and many working people were members of Friendly Societies, trade unions, insurance schemes, mutual aid societies and the like. Such self-help activities, combined with adult education and growing political enfranchisement, established even more clearly the gulf between such deserving respectable artisans and the residuum of paupers.

Poor Law provision was also supplemented by local authorities. Many towns and cities took it upon themselves to acquire powers to control the environment and regulate industry and trade within their boundary. Soon this extended to providing gas, water and light at public expense through the municipal rates, which led to the development by the 1880s and 1890s of the so-called gas and water socialism or municipal socialism. This co-existed with a continued faith in the values of individualism and self-help, and the contrast between ideology and practice was never better parodied than in Sidney Webb's famous story of the individualist town councillor who would:

> . . . walk along the municipal pavement, lit by municipal gas and cleansed by municipal brooms with municipal water, and seeing by the municipal clock in the municipal market that he is too early to meet his children coming from the municipal school, hard by the county lunatic asylum and municipal hospital, will use the national telegraph system to tell them not to walk through the municipal park, but to come by the municipal tramway to meet him in the municipal reading room by the municipal art gallery, museum and library where he intends to consult some of the national publications in order to prepare his next speech in the municipal town hall in favour of the nationalisation of canals and the increase of Government control over the railway system. 'Socialism, Sir', he will say, 'don't waste the time of a practical man by your fantastic absurdities. Self help, Sir, individual self help, that's what made our city what it is.'[2]

By this time poverty itself was to be conceived of in a new way. Charles Booth began a massive fifteen-year statistical survey of the East End of London from which he deduced a new way of thinking about social classes in Victorian England. Booth and his army of researchers and volunteers identified eight social groups of whom the lowest four were deemed to be in poverty. Booth's thinking and writing were part of a growing general understanding and redefinition of poverty from the 1880s onwards. The term 'unemployment' was first used in the 1880s, and gradually the environmental factors bearing upon individuals came to be seen as more important than their individual failings. Booth's work confirmed the causes of poverty beyond the control of the individual, low pay, unemployment, sickness, old age, etc. What shocked people, at the time, was the absolute level of poverty which he identified as over 30 per cent compared to the level of pauperism revealed in Poor Law statistics of under 3 per cent. As the economist Alfred Marshall told a Royal Commission, 'The problem of 1834 was pauperism, the problem of 1893 is poverty.'

It might have been thought that London, which Booth admitted had both the poorest and the richest sections of society, might be an exception and the evidence could not be generalised across the nation as a whole. In this respect a separate survey by the Quaker Seebohm Rowntree in York at the very end of the Victorian period was even more shocking because it demonstrated along the lines of the Booth inquiry that some 28 per cent of the population was in poverty. Rowntree's survey took the argument and methodology a stage further by distinguishing between primary and secondary poverty, the latter due to bad management of financial resources. Rowntree also identified the life-cycle of poverty, showing that there were stages in the typical family history when people would be in need.

The changes in the Poor Law, which made it by the end of Victoria's reign a specialised agency for the very poor and needy in particular social circumstances, contrasted sharply with these new revelations about poverty and its surprising extent. Some believed that a more enlightened Poor Law could indeed serve society well. For example, the reformer Canon Samuel Barnett, who worked tirelessly for the poor in the East End of London, wrote in 1883 that the Poor Law could be reformed 'so as to make the life of England healthier and more restful'. However, this was never likely to be the case given the deliberately enforced stigma attached to poor relief which had been at the heart of Poor Law practice for sixty years. Those in desperate need did have recourse to the Poor Law, but virtually all would have preferred to manage outside the Poor Law because of the punitive nature of the value system associated with it. This had been the deliberate intention and part of the overall strategy. Such a close association between pauperism and moral disfavour was reinforced by the way in which the newly identified sources of poverty, such as sickness and unemployment, were exempted from the full rigours of the workhouse or labour tests.

In the midst of a period of high unemployment and social disorder, the minister responsible for the Poor Law, Joseph Chamberlain, defined a new way of treating the unemployed. Chamberlain stressed that it was highly desirable that the general working-class distaste for the Poor Law should be maintained. The 1886 Chamberlain Circular stated:

> The spirit of independence which leads so many of the
> working classes to make great personal sacrifices rather than

incur the stigma of pauperism, is one which deserves the greatest sympathy and respect . . . It is not desirable that the working classes should be familiarised with poor relief.

What is required in the endeavour to relieve artisans and others who have hitherto avoided poor law assistance, and who are temporarily deprived of employment is work which will not involve the stigma of pauperism.[3]

Such thinking did not lead the Local Government Board, even in the light of Booth's and Rowntree's statistics, to seek to take the Poor Law away from its ideological origins. Hence, while political and social debate was contemplating an ever wider province for a positivist state, the Poor Law was virtually condemning itself to a backwater for the residuum. Popular distaste for the Poor Law, combined with its own policy imperatives, confirmed that as the new century opened, the broader social vision that was growing in strength would find its expression outside rather than inside the Poor Law of 1834.

THREE

The Emergence of a 'Social Service State' 1900–1939

In 1901 the long reign of Queen Victoria came to an end and she was succeeded by her son Edward VII, who gave his name to the image and culture of the pre-1914 age. At the time of his accession, Britain was at war in South Africa, and the Boer War began that intimate connection between war and welfare which characterised the first half of the twentieth century. The Boer War was started in 1899 as a very popular 'jingoistic' war supported by many volunteers. It surprised and worried British society to learn that up to one-third of all volunteers were rejected for military service on health grounds. This combined with growing worries about increased international economic competition from the USA and Germany and gave rise to ideas and debates about what came to be called 'national efficiency'. Darwinism spread into international relations with the idea that the fittest nations would survive, and in the international competition it was feared that Britain would be undermined by the deterioration of its human stock. Liberal Imperialists and Conservative tariff reformers alike came to the view that the state must take some action to remedy the potential decline in Britain's imperial greatness.

Other prominent strands of thought were pointing in a similar direction, most notably those arising from so-called New Liberals. These writers, politicians and journalists were inspired by the philosophy of idealism, which had developed from the 1880s under the influence of T.H. Green and Bernard Bosanquet. It transformed Gladstonian liberalism, with its emphasis upon economy and the free market, into a new form of liberalism which wished to use the state to secure national minimum conditions for all. J.A. Hobson talked about the state as 'over parent' and identified underconsumption among the working class as the key restraint upon economic and social development. Leonard Hobhouse, England's first Professor of Sociology, argued for the necessity of state action in order to encourage mutuality and spiritual regeneration.

Two important books in 1909 focused attention on the issues. Charles Masterman, himself a New Liberal MP, reviving a phrase much used in early Victorian England, wrote *The Condition of England*, advocating a major redistribution of wealth. In the same year, William Beveridge published *Unemployment, a Problem of Industry* in which he identified unemployment as an endemic feature of the industrial system and little to do with individual failings. These and other writings transformed thinking in Edwardian England from 'moralism' into 'causalism': from a broadly individualist perspective into a broadly collectivist perspective.

There were also strong socialist ideas being advocated in this period. The peculiarly British variant was Fabianism, best personified by Sidney and Beatrice Webb. The Fabian view equally supported a more interventionist state, but on different premises from that of New Liberalism. For the Fabians state intervention was less about moral reform of the individual and more about the almost Chadwickian faith in bureaucratic efficiency. Regulation, the rule of the expert, the enforcement of standard procedures and conditions would ensure the collective good of society. A collectivism based on regulation would replace an individualism based on *laissez-faire*. As one historian has put it, the Fabians represented 'mechanical reformism' and New Liberalism represented a 'moral reformism'.

Fabianism was certainly not the same as labourism and the Edwardian years saw a remarkable increase in the political self-identification of the Labour movement. The formal creation of the Labour Party and its pact with the Liberals led to a significant number of Labour MPs in the House of Commons following the landslide Liberal election of 1906. Labour was broadly socialistic, but by no means Marxist. It was by no means clear to the Labour movement that a newly empowered state, which would intervene in working-class lives, was the boon which New Liberals and Fabians advocated. Labour ideas were much more concerned with the spread of wealth to the generality of the population, so that individuals could make provision for themselves through their trade unions or friendly societies.

A key question was whether the Poor Law, which was the main state vehicle for the relief of social distress, could accommodate and respond to the new ideas for more collective rather than individual action. The reduction in the provision of outdoor relief to both men and women, which was common even in Labour-dominated areas such as Poplar and West Ham, was accompanied by an increase in the cost of Poor Relief as more paupers came to be relieved within institutions. While there was no reform of local finance and no equalisation of poor rates between rich and poor districts, the tendency would be to look to centralised state action and national finance to support any new social policy initiatives. In order to put this controversial political question on ice for a while, almost the last act of the outgoing Balfour government was to appoint, in 1905, a Royal Commission to look into the Poor Law. Just over seventy years after the Royal Commission had produced the New Poor Law, Edwardian Britain was given an opportunity to recast the Poor Law in a twentieth-century mould.

The Royal Commission was carefully chosen and encompassed the full spectrum of political and social opinion. It included politicians, central and local Poor Law administrators, representatives of New Liberal ideas, of Fabianism, and of Charity Organisation Society orthodoxy. There was even a socialist trade unionist on the Commission. More expert than the 1832 Commission, the 1905 Commission like its predecessor gathered a massive amount of research evidence and its work is a great quarry for Poor Law historians. It sat for over three years, but was unable to produce a unanimous report. The majority report of 1909, largely inspired by COS leader, Helen Bosanquet, wished to change the terminology of Poor Relief by the creation of public assistance committees, which would be a partnership between local government and the voluntary agencies. While acknowledging the strong environmental causes of poverty, illness and unemployment, the Majority Report still believed that at the heart of social distress lay moral failings which had to be remedied. The Minority Report, written by Beatrice Webb and her husband Sydney Webb, saw the moral failings associated with poverty as the consequence and not the cause of the social condition. The minority wanted a draconian and radical break-up of the Poor Law and its replacement by a series of specialised local bureaucracies under a registrar of public authority assistance. The Minority Report advocated a 'human sorting house' where people would be classified according to their potential and precise social condition. In true Fabian style, the Minority Report placed the expert at the heart of the proposed social security system.

It is interesting to note that, in an age when women lacked the parliamentary vote, it was the rivalry and opposition of two highly intelligent women, Helen Bosanquet and Beatrice Webb, that prevented the publication of a united report. The fact that these two women were backed by equally intelligent and important husbands has led to their description as 'an Edwardian mixed doubles'. Contemporary opinion was struck by the divisions between the two reports. Historians have been struck by how much they had in common. Both Minority and Majority Reports believed that the principles of 1834 were no longer appropriate. Both believed that relief should not be given without inquiry and proper classification. Both identified duplication between the Poor Law and local authorities and both proposed a prominent role for local authority provision. Both advocated rehabilitation and proper training and both had harsh things to say about the forcible extinction of the residuum.

It is tempting (though inaccurate) to see the Minority Report as an anticipation of a bureaucratically administered welfare state and the Majority Report as the restatement of reactionary views. What is more important is that the political leaders were not provided with a clear agenda for action. The result was that no reform of the Poor Law took place, notwithstanding the massive inquiry that had been conducted and the evident political and intellectual interest in these questions. The great reforms of the Liberal government between 1906 and 1914 can be seen, therefore, as a major turning point in the history of social policy, directed at reforming the social question outside the Poor Law and removing increasing numbers of potential clients from the Poor Law arena. In this sense the Poor Law was left to atrophy, as much of its remit was transferred to other agencies.

Well before the Royal Commission on the Poor Law had reported, the Liberal government had already made significant inroads into the free market. In the wake of the concerns arising from the Boer War, and fears of 'physical deterioration', free school meals were introduced in 1906 and in 1907 free school medical inspection. In both cases the responsible government agency was the Board of Education, and in neither case did the receipt of state help render the parents liable for poor relief with its associated stigma. In the 1908 Children Act, local authorities received significant central government financial subventions in order to provide for children in care and the state was confirmed as the ultimate guardian of child welfare. Some of this legislation was inspired by Labour and New Liberal backbench action and it may be correct to see these as minor encroachments. However, one contemporary writer imbued, for example, school meals with a major significance. 'The School Dinner is an education in citizenship. Without a word being said, the child gradually absorbs knowledge of its own dependence on and place in social life. He finds himself a guest at the common table of the nation.'

An even more significant innovation was the introduction of old-age pensions in 1908. Asquith as Chancellor had made provision for special expenditure and in 1908 it became possible to introduce non-contributory pensions, financed wholly out of central taxation, for those aged seventy or over who met an income limit test. Morality was not wholly dispensed with, for a criminal offence in the previous ten years or receipt of poor relief during the previous year disqualified the applicant. Yet at the same time there was a conscious attempt by Asquith 'to take the care of the aged and place it once and for all outside the machinery and association of our Poor Law system'. Payment of the old-age pension was to be through the Post Office, which further reinforced the distinction between an old-age pensioner and a pauper. Nearly half a million people qualified for the first tranche of old-age pensions, thus illustrating how much need there was in British society that was not being met by the Poor Law system.

Once it became clear that the Royal Commission on the Poor Law was not going to provide a political solution to the problems of work and health, then the way was open for alternative methods to be explored. Lloyd George (the Chancellor of the Exchequer, once Asquith became Prime Minister in 1908) made his famous visit to Germany in order to study the health insurance that had been introduced there by Bismarck. His 'People's Budget' in 1909 (which prompted a constitutional crisis with the House of Lords) was overtly redistributional in introducing a super tax for high incomes and a capital gains tax for land. The funding was therefore in place for a major intervention in the field of health care. The Treasury could not contemplate another non-contributory scheme, and insurance was seen as the answer for health care. Some of Lloyd George's more radical ideas, such as widows' and orphans' benefits, were dropped during the drafting of the Act. However, it was a significant change in the British way of life that those on incomes less than £160 per year would receive sick pay and free access to a GP. The scheme was to be financed by a 4*d* employee contribution, 3*d* employer's and 2*d* from the state. This was Lloyd George's popular redistributional slogan 'ninepence for fourpence'. Given the important and extensive role played by friendly societies and industrial insurance companies, the scheme was to be administered by approved societies, an interesting example of a partnership between state and voluntary action.

Part One of the National Insurance Act of 1911 was concerned with health and was the work of Lloyd George; Part Two was concerned with unemployment and was the work of Winston Churchill who had been influenced by William Beveridge. The latter was now put in charge of the innovation which he himself had recommended: the introduction of labour exchanges in 1909. By 1914 there were over

400 labour exchanges across the country financed by central taxation.

Other significant inroads into the free market were the concession in 1908 of an eight-hour day for miners, and the introduction of a minimum wage for miners in 1912. Similarly, trade boards were introduced in 1909 for the so-called sweated industries which established a minimum wage for some 500,000 workers, mainly women. Purists could accept some of these encroachments on the grounds that by this modest intervention the rest of the market economy could work more efficiently.

Unemployment remained a major scourge for most working people and, again, contemporary opinion had conceded that this was little to do with personal failing. Part Two of the 1911 National Insurance Act introduced a scheme to be administered by the Board of Trade and labour exchanges whereby some two and a quarter million people who worked in industries liable to fluctuation, such as construction, ship-building and engineering, were covered by an insurance scheme. Again based on employee/employer and state contribution, this entitled an unemployed worker to one week's benefit for every five contributions paid, up to a maximum of fifteen weeks.

By adopting the insurance principle for both health and unemployment the Liberal government hit upon a mechanism which had many advantages. First, there was the obvious financial point that it released sums of money and minimised the state taxation contribution. This was why much Labour opinion was opposed, on the grounds that the working class was required to pay for its own welfare. The second advantage was that it was a non-stigmatised form of relief based on entitlement, and this was reinforced by the payment of these benefits clearly outside the Poor Law. The final attraction was that the insurance principle confirmed the systematic, non-personal nature of the problems being dealt with. As Beveridge put it, unemployment insurance was a matter of 'industrial organisation' and in his phrase used the 'magic of averages' to provide the benefit, averaging the income of those in work with those out and averaging the benefit of those who were sick with those who were healthy. It removed the whole question of character (though elements of behavioural control still remained) and substituted the principle of citizenship. As Churchill said, 'I do not like mixing moralities and mathematics', and a recent historian has described it as securing social benefit 'through the solidarities of strangers'. There was no national plan or blue-print for the Liberal government which inspired the broad-ranging social programme, yet Churchill and Lloyd George, at least, saw, perhaps dimly, that these experiments could be built upon for a broader social purpose. Churchill talked about 'the universal establishment of minimum standards of life and labour' and Asquith described the National Insurance Act as 'the greatest alleviation of the risks and sufferings of life that parliament had conferred upon any people'. In such statements is the kernel of the idea of the social service state which was created in Britain before the First World War.

The First World War was itself a great catalyst for a massive expansion in the state's role, and, while some activities were clearly emergency war-time measures, there would be no turning back after the First World War to an individualist *laissez-faire* philosophy. The Defence of the Realm Act in 1914 gave to the government draconian powers to control and direct both material and human resources. Compulsory conscription was introduced in 1915 and, in mobilising resources for a total war, the government took on new and extensive powers. There was a fundamental shift in economic power as full employment, for the first time, gave to the working class an unprecedented potential influence over policy. Trade union membership doubled from four million to eight million during the war and it was the strength of working-class solidarity which led to the unprecedented control of rents in 1915. A series of rent strikes in 'Red Clydeside' forced the government to introduce this novel interference in the rights of property.

In the bitter political battle which led in 1916 to the replacement of Asquith as Prime Minister by Lloyd George, which effectively split the Liberal Party, there was an opportunity for the radical Liberal, Lloyd George, not only to fight the war more vigorously, but to return to the social questions on which he had made his reputation before 1914. Lloyd George recognised the dramatically destabilising effect of the First World War and the possibilities of regeneration. He set up in 1917 a Ministry of Reconstruction to plan a major social programme for the postwar years. What gave added edge to this question was the fear of

Bolshevism, particularly in the wake of the Russian Revolution of 1917. It is now known that the government received regular reports from police agents evaluating the state of working-class opinion. Lloyd George was advised that as far as Bolshevism was concerned, and its support among the working class, 'the government's determination to push forward with an advanced social programme is the best antidote'. Housing was always a key working-class issue and Lloyd George captured the spirit of the age by his (perhaps unwise) promise of 'Homes Fit For Heroes'. This led at the end of the war to the landmark Housing and Town Planning Act of 1919, which laid a duty upon local authorities to provide houses and provided a generous subsidy for council house building. Under this and subsequent legislation, Britain built far more municipal houses than any other western country. Lloyd George remained Prime Minister until 1922, but his ambitious radical programme of social reform foundered on the rocks of financial crisis, once the postwar costs began to fall upon the Treasury.

Initially there were high hopes for postwar reform through the creation of a united Ministry of Health in 1918, which brought together the Local

Government Board, and with it the Poor Law, and
the National Health Insurance scheme. In practice,
there were no dramatic changes in health policy
during the inter-war years, though by incremental
improvements, the health insurance scheme
became established for perhaps half the population.
By the beginning of the Second World War a clear
pattern had emerged of basic GP provision for male
and female insured workers, but with no coverage
for their dependants. Because a significant role was
given to the approved societies in the original 1911
scheme, the variable wealth and success of the
societies meant variable benefits for their members.
In particular, optical, dental and hospital services
were provided only by the most affluent approved
societies. Hospital treatment was still essentially a
service provided by the voluntary hospitals and the
local authority maintained hospital services. Beyond
health insurance, there were some improvements in
the maternity and child welfare, run by local
authorities, and similarly the local authorities'
environmental health services were much extended
in this period.

There were more significant changes in the field
of pensions. Neville Chamberlain, the most impor-

tant Conservative government social reformer during this period, was determined to extend what he saw as a minimal, but costly, scheme begun in 1908. There was no funding to extend a non-contributory scheme and the widely desired objective of reducing pensionable age to sixty-five was only feasible in the context of a general contributory pension scheme. Under the 1925 Old Age, Widows and Orphans Contributory Pensions Act, pensions were granted to men and women aged between sixty-five and sixty-nine under the National Health Insurance Scheme. Coverage was also extended to widows and orphans. It was anticipated that over time the contributory scheme would overtake the non-contributory, which would gradually die out.

The issue which came to dominate the whole inter-war period was unemployment. Once the post-war boom had ended, unemployment topped a million by the end of 1920 and it was never below a million until war broke out in 1939, at times being as high as 3 million. Unemployment cast a dark shadow over the whole inter-war period as both cyclical and structural unemployment reached unprecedented levels, particularly in the industrial heartland. Employment in coal fell by 35 per cent during these years, in cotton by 40 per cent, in iron and steel by 35 per cent, and in shipbuilding by over 50 per cent.

Government response to this crisis was unplanned, *ad hoc* and lacked any coherent logic or system. The hope always was that the unemployed worker could be given non-pauperised relief, while at the same time preserving the actuarial principles of insurance. The more the state was forced to subsidise (and even bail out) a flawed and deficient insurance scheme, the more the unemployment problem would come to the heart of government by challenging the basis of government expenditure as a whole. Unemployment insurance which had begun as a scheme restricted to specific industries was broadly generalised in the years after the war, as this was deemed appropriate reward for the heroes who had fought in the trenches. Yet as soon as unemployment topped the million mark the actuarial basis of the insurance scheme became undermined. From the early 1920s the principle was introduced of so-called 'uncovenanted benefit' which, in effect, paid unemployment benefit to workers on the basis of supposed future contributions. Later expedients were Transitional Benefit or

Extended Benefit, which covered the gaps in insurance coverage, and inevitably increased the government's subsidy.

As a defence mechanism against possible fraud, the 1920s introduced the expedient of 'the genuinely seeking work test', echoes of which are still with us today. For those claiming either uncovenanted or transitional benefits (i.e. benefit to which the claimant was not strictly entitled by contributions), the applicant had to prove that they were genuinely seeking work and had made every endeavour to find it. Few people seriously believed there was ever enough work for all to find. However, the effects of 'the genuinely seeking work test' were demonstrated by the fact that between 1920 and 1929, when it was abolished by the Labour government, some 3 million people were deprived of benefit on the basis of this test. It was hardly surprising that its abolition became one of the main electoral demands of the Labour Party as it fought the 1929 election.

'The genuinely seeking work test' was detested by working people, but it was to be overtaken in public contempt by the 'family means test' which was introduced as a consequence of the crisis of the early 1930s. One of the aims of the various insurance expedients of the 1920s was to protect workers from the stigma of poor relief. This was no less important to the applicant who, as it were, applied with his cap on for benefit, but with his cap off for relief. *In extremis*, the unemployed workman did have to apply to the Poor Law, and in the wake of the General Strike, for example, the numbers on poor relief soared. The spirit of 1834 was not wholly dead, and guardians, particularly in Labour areas with high unemployment, were reminded that even in times of distress the level of relief 'should of necessity be calculated on a lower scale than the earnings of the independent labourer who is maintaining himself by his labour'. Baldwin's Conservative government of the later 1920s was particularly worried about the growing number of Poor Law Unions that were dominated by Labour politicians, and by Neville Chamberlain's 1929 Local Government Act, the Poor Law Guardians and the Unions were finally swept away after nearly one hundred years of existence. By a strange irony, Labour MPs fought a rearguard action to defend the Poor Law Union, because, as a separately elected body, it gave some prospect of working people controlling the benefits system.

fell, though unemployment never disappeared, and was regarded throughout the period as a blight on the nation. Meanwhile, the combination of health insurance, widows', old-age and orphans' pensions, unemployment insurance, the growth of local authority social services (such as welfare clinics and school medical inspection), housing development and other social measures did, in a rather haphazard way, nevertheless increase social expenditure quite dramatically in these years. It has been estimated that there was a five-fold increase in expenditure on social services between 1918 and 1938: in 1918 such expenditure accounted for 2.4 per cent of gross national product and by 1938 that had become 11.3 per cent. Yet there was a growing feeling arising out of the many social surveys carried out in the period, that more was needed and a broader social policy could be justified in the national interest. The welfare system of 1939 was a patchwork quilt, with some bright hues among other areas of indeterminate colour and even with rents and holes within it. Even the most generous of state insurance benefits were not deemed to be at a level of subsistence, but were intended to supplement personal savings and individual provision. Such an approach was gradually being countered by the idea of maintenance according to need, the evidence for which grew out of the extensive social investigation and knowledge of social conditions in the 1920s and 1930s. Such ideas never got beyond the planning and debating stage in times of peace, and it was significant that they only finally bore fruit in times of war.

FOUR

The Creation of the British Welfare State, 1940–1948

The relationship between war and welfare which characterised the first half of the twentieth century reached its most intensive phase during the Second World War. The coincidence of military technology which made bombing and air raids the distinctive feature of the Second World War, together with the demands of total war which made this genuinely a People's War, combined to put the social position of the British population at the very heart of the war effort. The first experience of war for most families was the evacuation of their children at the outbreak of war. The imposition of largely urban, working-class children upon largely provincial and rural middle-class families exposed, in a way that none of the social surveys could, the true deprivation that still characterised broad swathes of British society. A growing climate of social solidarity was further reinforced by bombing and food shortages, which affected rich and poor alike. The ration book became a great symbol of fair shares and fair sacrifice for all, while, as in the First World War, there was a massive extension of state control of industry, conscription and the direction of labour.

There were some important practical and symbolic developments, particularly after May 1941 when Churchill became Prime Minister of a coalition government and the phoney war was over. Provision of school meals was extended so that by the end of the war ten times as many children were taking them than at the beginning of the war; school milk and subsidised milk were provided for infants and pregnant women; the famous wartime orange juice, vitamins and cod liver oil were widely distributed. These basic social questions were addressed with a new vigour and determination, which compared starkly with the lack of concern during the 1930s. The Unemployment Assistance Board was renamed the Assistance Board and had a much broader remit to include those dislocated through the war, as well as displaced persons and refugees. Supplementary pensions were introduced, paid according to need, and under the influence of Ernest Bevin, the trade union leader brought into the coalition government, the hated household means test was replaced with a much softer and more sympathetic assumption of certain family income.

One of the most significant developments was the creation of the wartime Emergency Medical Service which, in effect, temporarily nationalised all hospital services under a coherent and planned service, in anticipation of mass disruption and injury through bombing. The Emergency Medical Service revealed the diversity of provision and the geographical unevenness of hospital and medical services which were to be an important stimulus in the creation of a National Health Service. In a very wide range of social, economic and administrative interventions, the British State took on a much broader role in the interests of the successful prosecution of what was a total war of unprecedented social impact. It was, in short, a war in which a citizen army was mobilised, part of which fought overseas and an equally important part of which was working in factories, mines and other war-related industries and serving in the Home Guard.

The war had a radicalising effect upon much opinion, and the fact that it was an ideological war forced people to consider what they were fighting for. If the Depression years of the thirties, with their painful memories of mass unemployment, were not to be repeated, then a new social and political order would have to be created. As early as the summer of 1940, the voice of the establishment, *The Times* newspaper, produced an editorial which captured the changed political climate:

> If we speak of democracy, we do not mean a democracy which maintains the right to vote, but forgets the right to work and the right to live. If we speak of freedom, we do not mean a rugged individualism which excludes social organisation and economic planning. If we speak of equality, we do not mean a political equality nullified by social and economic privilege. . . . The new order cannot be based upon the preservation of privilege whether the privilege be that of a country, of a class or of an individual.[4]

Perhaps more significant was the 1941 New Year edition of *Picture Post* which comprised a whole issue devoted to 'a plan for Britain'. The chapters discussed educational reform and an end of class

distinctions, housing and town planning, the relief
of poverty, a free health service and many other
aspects of a new and ideal society. The magazine
commented, 'Our plan for the new Britain is not
something outside the war, or something *after* the
war. It is an essential part of our war aims. It is,
indeed, our most positive war aim. The new Britain
is the country we are fighting for.'

It was in this context of a willingness to contemplate fundamental social and political change and in
a climate of radical national solidarity, created, no
doubt temporarily and artificially, by the necessities
of war, that the Beveridge Report was written. It was
at once both the product of, and the articulation of,
the radical social democracy of the war years. In
retrospect, as at the time, it was the most potent
symbol of wartime aspirations for a better world.
Beveridge himself became a popular hero, with both
contemporaries and historians commenting on how
unlikely a hero he was and how the origin of the
report was far less heroic than its eventual outcome.
Beveridge had played an important part in the
development of social and economic policy before
and during the First World War. Thereafter he had
been the Director of the London School of

conomics and in the later thirties became a Master of an Oxford College. This was hardly the background of a popular wartime hero. When war began Beveridge was drawn into the government service, but felt frustrated that his main talent, which he felt lay in manpower planning, was not being fully exploited.

There was a widespread acceptance that the chaotic and disorganised schemes of social insurance, that involved no less than seven government departments and a myriad of insurance and other schemes, were in need of some rationalisation. And when it was decided that a minor committee of civil servants would be established to review the regime of social insurance Bevin, who found Beveridge a nuisance, decided that Beveridge should chair the committee. Beveridge later reported that there were tears in his eyes because of the disappointment at not getting a more important job than to chair this committee which would look at Social Insurance and Allied Services.

By sheer force of personality, dedication and no little inspiration, Beveridge was able to turn this potentially insignificant committee into a major engine of social reform. His civil servant advisers from the relevant departments, including the Treasury, soon became alarmed at the ideas Beveridge was expressing and by the end of 1941 it was agreed that the report would be signed by Sir William Beveridge himself alone, for fear of committing civil servants and the government to any of his alarming and outlandish ideas. In the winter of 1941/2, fully a year before the Beveridge Report appeared, the Chairman had written heads of a scheme which more or less established the structure and broad content of his report. A bit like Chadwick in the 1830s, Beveridge had broadly come to his conclusions before he had studied all the evidence, and the 127 witnesses who appeared before the committee during 1942 were, in effect, commenting on points of detail. Beveridge went way beyond his terms of reference to create a powerful document, which argued the case for a coherent social and economic policy which would conduce to the welfare of the whole British people.

Though overtly a Liberal, an image reinforced by his position briefly as a Liberal MP at the end of the war, Beveridge at this time was moving towards a strong almost socialistic belief in planning and economic control. Much influenced by John

Maynard Keynes, whose theories of demand management appeared to be fulfilled by the effects of war in reviving the British economy and curing the problem of unemployment, Beveridge was willing to countenance a very broad compass for the modern state which would act across a much broader canvass than previously. This report was published in December 1942 and captured this broad framework by, in Bunyanesque terms, describing the need to destroy five giants on the road to reconstruction – Want, Ignorance, Disease, Squalor and Idleness. Although the report would deal in detail only with Want, the coherence of the social policies envisaged by the image of the five giants have set the broad limits of what later came to be called the Welfare State.

The language of the five giants captured the public imagination, but Beveridge's use of the term Assumptions was equally important. He argued that no effective system of social security could operate unless three Assumptions were met; Assumption A was family allowances; Assumption B was a free health service and Assumption C was the maintenance of employment, the avoidance of mass unemployment. By classifying these profound and radical innovations as merely Assumptions, Beveridge deemed them obvious and essential prerequisites, requiring no special justification. The Beveridge Plan, as it became known, was based upon a number of simple principles. Social security would be universal and comprehensive, for it would cover all persons and all insurable risks. No longer would social relief be simply 'reserved for the poor', for the whole of the British population would be encompassed within the social security scheme. Everyone, according to their insurance classification, would pay a single flat-rate contribution which would earn a contractual entitlement to adequate flat rate benefits. Since all of the normal interruptions to income in a normal life could be anticipated, then insurance would bear the risk in a common pool for all people to meet all eventualities. As the phrase had it, it would cover people from the cradle to the grave, or alternatively from the crib to the coffin.

Beveridge drew on the many developments which had taken place since the beginning of the century and also drew on ideas and proposals which had been widely circulated in the late 1930s. He argued therefore that it was a typical British revolution drawing the best of the past into a new future; but he was in no doubt that it was, indeed, a revolution and he argued that this was no time for patching, but for taking a decisive new turn in the history of social policy. Beveridge envisaged that all normal contingencies could be met through insurance, and he anticipated that for those who would be outside the insurance scheme, through the lack of contributions or through an inability to participate in the normal economy, there would be a means tested residual national assistance service funded wholly out of taxation. Such assistance, however, would be provided with more behavioural conditions, for, as Beveridge wrote, 'an assistance scheme which makes those assisted unamenable to economic rewards or punishments while treating them as free citizens is inconsistent with the principles of a free community'.

There were 300 pages of closely argued and highly technical words in the Beveridge Report, yet it became a bestseller. There has never been an official report before or since that has had such a wide readership or such a broadly based appeal, both within the country and, perhaps even more significantly, in countries abroad. Over 600,000 copies of the report were sold, and Beveridge appeared on the radio, newsreels and in the press. To his great surprise he acquired the celebrity of a film star or a popular musician. Public opinion polls found that nineteen out of twenty people had heard of the Beveridge Report and almost all were in favour of its implementation. 'Beveridge Now' was the cry. In a unique set of circumstances, Beveridge had managed to capture the spirit of the age and express within a plan for social policy the aspirations of a whole generation for a better society for their children.

In the nearly six decades since the appearance of the Beveridge Report opinion has shifted from this initial euphoria. There is, indeed, a marked contrast between the popular enthusiasm for and acceptance of the Beveridge Report at the time and the views now expressed by social scientists and social historians. Indeed, the leading historian of social policy since the Second World War (Lowe) now describes the Beveridge Report as 'an ineffective and conservative document', while a fellow historian (Digby) refers to the report as 'an ambiguous and eclectic document that was less bedrock than shifting sand'. Abel Smith, a leading poverty scholar, comments that 'the report was in many ways flawed and failed to live up to its promises'.

Why do these scholars see deficiencies in Beveridge that were clearly not perceived in the first flush of popular acclaim at the time? Leaving aside the general issue of whether the Beveridge Report generated a misplaced and extravagant imperative in postwar policy (which is discussed later), the critics of Beveridge have identified four main flaws in his proposals. It can be argued that there is some merit in the first two, but the latter two are based almost wholly on hindsight.

The first criticism concerns the fact that Beveridge never fully bottomed out the problem of the poverty line, though this was not for want of trying. One of the critical elements in the Beveridge Plan was that benefits should be adequate and meet subsistence needs. The central problem was the question of rent. Beveridge freely acknowledged that rent varied across the country, and he was also aware that means-tested benefits had often included the actual rent paid. In the event, however, he decided on the grounds of simplicity and to preserve the social insurance principle, that rents should be averaged. Inevitably, then, some recipients would be inadequately treated while others would be relatively generously treated. Subsequent analytical studies

71

suggest that Beveridge himself set the subsistence levels too low and that wartime inflation eroded those levels still further.

The second criticism highlights the way in which the Beveridge Report simultaneously had philosophical and psychological strengths, but administrative and technical weaknesses. One of the most profound psychological attractions for the British people in the Beveridge Plan was the principle of flat-rate contributions and flat-rate benefits. In this simple proposition was encapsulated the whole ethos of fair shares for all and the principle of contractual entitlement to the benefits received.

Beveridge did consider using the widely accepted European practice of earnings-related contributions and benefits, but he rejected them on the grounds that the flat-rate principle was a powerful call to arms for social justice. He also questioned whether it was reasonable for the state to provide for a standard of living above subsistence: that was the province of individual and voluntary endeavour. Yet what was attractive in terms of its social acceptability (in stark contrast to the popular hatred of means-tested benefits) had a fundamental problem, sometimes in wartime language referred to as the convoy principle. The speed of a convoy was that of the slowest ship, so the level of flat-rate contributions would be determined by that which was affordable to the lowest wage earner. In turn, this limited the fund which could be built up by insurance contributions and consequentially limited the levels of benefits that could be paid. Both the flat-rate principle and the studies on subsistence do reveal shortcomings in the Beveridge approach, but he believed (and many have believed since) that the advantages in philosophy, social acceptance and contractual entitlement outweighed the technical shortcomings.

The third sort of criticism is somewhat less precise, but centres on the alleged lack of a dynamic quality in Beveridge's proposals. Beveridge has been criticised, along with Keynes, for solving the problems of the thirties and not of the postwar years. The simplicity and uniformity of the Beveridge Plan was not well suited to the diverse needs which were to develop in later decades and it has been argued that what was needed was a much more flexible, responsive policy which could have been much better tuned to individual need as it developed. Though the product of a time of change, the Beveridge Report has been criticised for not anticipating the changes that would come about in the postwar world. The Report failed to include fiscal and occupational welfare and did not attempt to link benefit and taxation regimes. These criticisms rely on Beveridge's understandable inability to predict the future.

Similarly, the fourth main criticism has something of a hindsight critique about it and has been associated with the growth of feminism. In his day Beveridge was thought to be, and believed himself to be, a progressive as far as women's rights were concerned. He was, indeed, an early proponent of what we would now call equal opportunities. There is much in the Report that acknowledges the value of women as home-makers and carers, and there was a proposal for a separate 'housewives' charter'. A leading women's activist at the time said that Beveridge had 'gone a long way towards establishing the rights of a married woman as a worker and as a partner in the home.' However, Beveridge found it difficult to incorporate women into a contributory insurance scheme. He believed that seven out of eight married women would not work and that therefore their insurance benefit should be derived mainly through their husbands. Of course, in the decades following the war there were many social and demographic changes which changed the position of women. Far more women, including married women, did take up employment, there were more single parent families, more divorces, and the feminist movement has generally given the Beveridge Report a hard time for his alleged conservatism in reinforcing outdated modes of family life. Because the notion of citizenship was closely tied up with the notion of social insurance, those who were effectively outside social insurance or not well served by it were thereby deemed to be deprived of all or part of their citizen entitlement.

The fact that on all of these issues it is possible to take a different view of the same evidence merely reinforces the point which Beveridge's biographer has made, that the report was a portmanteau of ideas in which everyone could find something to support. Politically Liberals could identify with the notions of freedom and the Liberal lineage back to the days of Lloyd George. Conservatives could admire the underlying faith in the free market and the continued reference to the need for personal individual provision above the minimum. And Labour, to whom it fell to implement the Beveridge

Plan, found in the Beveridge Report social justice and the prospect of more equitable society for which the party had been created.

Government reaction at the time also drew a sharp contrast with the popular enthusiasm. Senior civil servants and government ministers had resented the way Beveridge had ignored the conventions of official reports and they also resented what they saw as the cult of personality which Beveridge was encouraging. Beveridge and his allies had engineered what we would now call a public relations coup, which clearly placed the Churchill government on the defensive. Churchill personally had developed an animosity for Beveridge, notwithstanding their alliance during the Edwardian years. He took the view that the war was far from over and that such talk of a possibly undeliverable panacea was too reminiscent of the painful betrayal associated with 'Homes fit for heroes' after the First World War. Churchill was in no doubt that the first priority had to be winning the war and plans for reconstruction would have to take very much a second place. Moreover, the coalition government, including Labour ministers, were not wholly convinced by the contents of the Beveridge Plan, and senior civil servants, particularly from the Treasury, encouraged a degree of scepticism.

In a debate which began at the time and has, in various forms, gone on ever since, the Beveridge Plan was denounced by senior civil servants under Treasury influence as extravagant and unaffordable and potentially creating a major burden on future postwar economic investment. Even at the time there were divided views on the facts of the matter. Beveridge had, in fact, made great efforts to ensure that his Report was fully costed and affordable. In discussions with Keynes six months before the Report was finished, Beveridge had agreed to some economies which would make the plan even more financially secure. He had agreed to exclude from family allowances the first child and he also agreed to make the full old-age pension payable over a transition period of twenty years. Keynes, in fact, said 'the Chancellor of the Exchequer should thank his stars that he has got off so cheap'. And members of the economic section of the Treasury believed that the Beveridge Plan was actually cheaper than the previous provision.

To be sure, 'Beveridge Now' was not a practical proposition, for there were many technical questions which had to be addressed. However, such logic led to the widespread suspicion that the government was lukewarm on Beveridge and when the Report came up for its official parliamentary debate in February 1943 there was the largest single vote against the coalition government during the whole war. Ninety-seven Labour MPs were among those who voted for an amendment calling for the immediate implementation of Beveridge, and the impression was indelibly created upon public opinion that it was the Labour Party that would be more likely to implement the Beveridge Plan. Many Labour activists firmly believed that the outcome of the next election was determined by that vote in February 1943.

There was no alternative but to plan for legislation that would be implemented after the war, and the coalition government developed a series of White Papers in the wake of the Beveridge proposals. It was these White Papers rather than the Beveridge Report itself which, in effect, became the blue-print for subsequent legislation. The White Paper, *Social Insurance* (1944) broadly accepted Beveridge's proposals and was both universal and comprehensive in its coverage. Echoing the radical wartime spirit which had sustained the Beveridge Report, the

White Paper referred to 'the solidarity and unity of the nation which in war have been its bulwark against aggression and in peace will be its guarantee of success in the fight against individual want and mischance'. The White Paper was less certain than Beveridge had been about the adequacy of benefits and referred to a 'reasonable level', which was the formula to be introduced in the subsequent legislation.

Earlier in the same year the government had produced its White Paper on *Employment Policy* which showed how far official thinking had moved towards Keynesian economics and a consequent commitment to use public expenditure to maintain a high level of employment. This White Paper had been rushed out in order to forestall what was billed as a second Beveridge Report that was eventually published as a book called *Full Employment in a Free Society*. Beveridge had been isolated from government circles, and his book is a more radical clarion call for Keynesian demand management and full employment. Yet, even before these two White Papers had appeared, the government had responded to Beveridge's Assumption B and had produced a White Paper, *A National Health Service*,

which indicated all-party agreement for a comprehensive service covering all branches of medical
activity.

The all-party agreement which enabled the coalition government to introduce such far-reaching
plans was stretched to the limit on the question of
land and housing. The 1944 White Paper on *Control
of Land Use* sought to steer a middle way between
Conservative faith in the free market with proper
compensation for compulsory purchase and the
Labour commitment to the nationalisation of land.
Nevertheless, there was agreement on the general
principles of planning and the wartime newly found
faith in planned development was admirably
captured in the words of the White Paper:

> Provision for the right use of land, in accordance with a
> considered policy, is an essential requirement of the
> government's programme of post war reconstruction. New
> houses . . . the new layout of areas devastated by enemy
> action . . . the new schools which will be required . . . the
> balanced distribution of industry . . . the preservation of
> land for national parks and forests . . . a new and safer
> highway system . . . all these related parts of a single
> reconstruction programme involved the use of land, and it

is essential that their various claims on land should be so
harmonised as to ensure for the people of this country the
greatest possible measure of individual well-being and
national prosperity.[5]

The same spirit was to be found in the legislation
around education. A White Paper, *Educational
Reconstruction*, in 1943 had been broadly supported,
and it was widely anticipated that a major education
act could be implemented before the end of the
war. This White Paper was the basis of the 1944
Education Act introduced by R.A. Butler, which laid
the foundation for the major expansion in
educational provision which occurred in the
postwar decades. Under the Act a Ministry of
Education was established, and the duty laid upon
the Minister of providing a comprehensive national
educational system. The modern divisions of
primary, secondary and further education were
introduced and fee-paying was abolished at all local
education authority schools. The school-leaving age
was to be raised to fifteen, with a promise of a
further raising to sixteen later on. The Act laid
down that there should be parity of esteem between
all types of educational provision. Although it did

not abolish public schools, as some Labour activists wished, nor did it end the influence of religion and voluntary schools in the English state system, nevertheless the 1944 Education Act represented a high point for democratic consensus in wartime and was a potent symbol of the people's war.

The final product of the wartime consensus was the introduction, without opposition, of the Family Allowances Act in 1945. Eleanor Rathbone had led a long campaign going back to the beginning of the century based on arguments about family endowment, reaction to child poverty and demographic incentives. In the event, it was the exigencies of war which finally created the impetus for the introduction of family allowances. Assumption A of the Beveridge Report was implemented at a somewhat lower rate than Beveridge had recommended, which was justified by the increase in other state provisions that were either already enacted or promised. Beveridge saw family allowances as an essential means of preserving the flatrate principles of social insurance, while recognising family need. For him, family allowances permitted the maintenance of work incentives while paying subsistence-level benefits, ensuring that even the low paid received a subsistence income. Employers saw this as the lesser evil in the face of the possibilities of the minimum wage or statutory imposition of wage increases, and trade unionists finally dropped their opposition to what had previously been regarded as a means of preserving low wages.

By the later stages of the war, there was widespread agreement that reconstruction, physical and social, was now the highest priority as Britain prepared for peace. Few of the plans or enactments were wholly original, for all had been widely debated in the 1930s and in the early war years. What the war and the Beveridge Report created, however, was the raised expectation and the political democratic will for these to be implemented. There were many doubters about the wisdom of the priority given to social reconstruction, but there was a political imperative which could not be resisted and which was to find the fullest expression at the 1945 election. Perhaps the two most well-known and well-regarded individuals in Britain in 1945 were Winston Churchill and William Beveridge, yet both had their political hopes dashed in the 1945 election. The Conservative Party was swept away in a landslide victory for Labour and the short-lived political career of Beveridge as a Liberal MP came to an end when he was defeated. It was Clement Attlee as Prime Minister in 1945 whose responsibility it was to reward the British people for their wartime efforts and to create the so-called 'new Jerusalem' of the Welfare State.

This was the first Labour government to have a majority, and Labour ministers were acutely conscious that their new found political power should be put to radical social purpose. The highest priority was to deliver on the Beveridge Report. James Griffiths, who had led the Labour revolt in February 1943, was appropriately in charge of the National Insurance Act of 1946. This was true to the Beveridge vision and encompassed the whole population in a single comprehensive insurance scheme. For a single flat-rate insurance contribution, people received, depending upon their insurance classification, benefits from the cradle to the grave. As the *Daily Mail* explained it in 1948, there was a new Britain 'which takes over its citizens six months before they are born, providing care and free services for their birth, for their early years, their schooling, sickness, workless days, widowhood and retirement'. There was little controversy about the National Insurance Act since it followed so closely on the Beveridge Report and the White Paper of 1944. However, there was a back-bench Labour protest at the time limit imposed on unemployment benefit, which had not been part of the Beveridge Plan (though it had proposed that benefit beyond six months would be conditional upon training). The levels of benefit were higher than Beveridge recommended, but subsequent studies have estimated that wartime inflation left the 1946 benefit levels about 10 per cent lower than Beveridge had intended. One improvement on Beveridge, which had already been agreed by the coalition government, was to pay the increased retirement pensions immediately and not wait for the twenty years of transition. The new levels of pension were paid from October 1946, soon after the first family allowances were also paid, thus requiring positive support from the Chancellor of the Exchequer, Hugh Dalton.

Also in 1946, Griffiths introduced the National Insurance Industrial Injuries Act which removed the question of workmen's compensation from the whole area of litigation and dispute. It was an interesting comment on the values of the 1940s that industrial injuries, alongside injuries suffered in war service, were to be covered at a benefit level that was higher than national insurance payments. The Beveridge Report had also referred to the need for a non-insurance based safety net, and this was provided by the National Assistance Act of 1948 which formally ended the legislative life of the Poor Law. The National Assistance Board would provide support for those who lacked entitlement to insurance benefits and for those whose insurance benefits did not meet their actual needs. In this taxation-based system, it was assumed, both in 1942 and in 1948, that in time the need for such service would dramatically decline. In practice, partly because of the level of inflation and because of the issue of rents which were payable under National Assistance, the NAB levels of benefit could be higher than those earned by National Insurance, but it was argued that National Assistance was a means-tested benefit and would therefore be paid only to those in genuine need.

Assumption C of the Beveridge Report, the commitment to full employment, was certainly honoured by the Labour government. There was a major programme of nationalisation of industry and

was approved by the Labour cabinet,
rearguard action by Herbert Morrison in
the local authorities. Bevan was equally
t he would not contemplate the sale of
ractices and he was anxious to ensure that
an adequate and reasonable distribution of
ervices across the country, which could be
only by some degree of government
although the Conservatives voted against
nal Health Service Act of 1946, the main
sy about the implementation of this
n lay not inside Parliament, but outside,
ly with the doctors themselves. Both the
dical Association (BMA) and the various
eges had agreed that some sort of national
rvice should be created. However, the
ractitioners in particular were obsessively
l and fearful about the creation of a full-
ied service. They regarded themselves as
yed contractors and argued that a salaried
th its socialistic tendencies, contained a
heir medical independence. Bevan never
o create a salaried service, though he did
the salaries of doctors should be a
on between a salaried element and a

services, the use of Keynesian methods to maintain
the level of demand and strong economic planning
and control. Apart from a severe winter in 1946/7
(the worst of the century), unemployment was at or
below 2 per cent, below the level which both Keynes
and Beveridge had deemed to be full employment. If
Want and Idleness had been effectively dealt with by
the Labour Government, there was less success with
two other of the Beveridge giants, Ignorance and
Squalor. The main legislative framework for
education had already been set by the Butler Act and
it was for Labour to implement the proposals under
that scheme. The school leaving-age was raised to
fifteen in 1947. Schools were built (notwithstanding
shortage of raw materials and a highly stretched
construction industry), local authorities did deliver
their education plans, and for the first time the mass
of British children were able to have free secondary
education. Yet few nursery schools were built, and
there was less progress in further and technical
education than had been hoped for. It was under
Labour that the eleven-plus and the tripartite
division between grammar, secondary modern and
technical schools became fully established in the
British educational system.

Educational reformers would have liked to have gone further, and a similar sense of missed opportunities was associated with housing policy. There were, of course, massive difficulties in rebuilding Britain after the war. Again there were some successes. The 1946 New Towns Act made possible the designation of fourteen new towns to act as overspill and the 1947 Town & Country Planning Act ensured that the community rather than individual private landlords enjoyed the profits from improved land values for development. The government favoured the local authority over private developers, and the ambitious housing targets promised in the 1945 election were not delivered. Nevertheless, some one million houses were built during the period of the Labour government, despite financial crises and construction difficulties. The quality of these houses was certainly an improvement, but there was clearly a demand for quantity which the Labour government's achievements were not able to match.

No such criticism can be levelled at the central plank of the Welfare State which was the creation of the National Health Service, Beveridge's Assumption B. It is tempting to see the creation of the NHS as a

foregone conclusion.
dissatisfaction with tl
developed in the 1930
seen promises made by
National Health Serv
Beveridge Report gave
ency and the White Pa
clear commitment to t
vice. However, for all tl
was, in fact, no clear a
holders on some key ci
of a national service
shape, organisation ar
been fully worked th
Aneurin Bevan, the yo
government, was the
implement a National
Bevan immediately
wartime plans were
almost wholly unex
nationalise all volunta
This immediately deal
the rivalry between
authority hospitals an
authority control. The

hospital
despite a
favour o
clear tha
medical
there was
medical s
achieved
control.
the Natic
controve
legislatio
particula
British M
Royal Co
health se
general
concerne
time sala
self-empl
service,
threat to
intended
feel that
combina

capitation element. Nevertheless, in an unedifying political battle between Bevan and the doctors, this issue along with questions of medical discipline and direction of labour, dominated an increasingly bitter war of words between the two.

As late as February 1948, only a few months before the NHS was due to start, seven out of eight GPs said in a BMA ballot that they would not join the new service. In the end, through great political skill, Bevan was able to forge an alliance with the consultants who, having negotiated for themselves a privileged and rewarding position within the new NHS, then became strong allies of Bevan in bringing the BMA and the general practitioners round to accept the service. The breakthrough came, finally, when at the suggestion of the consultants, Bevan conceded that a salaried service would require separate special legislation, and with this assurance the doctors fell into line. What Bevan created was a tripartite structure, with enormous power vested in the Minister: 14 regional hospital boards oversaw the hospital services; 140 executive councils delivered the general medical services, together with dental, pharmaceutical and ophthalmic services; and 146 local health authorities provided ancillary services such as health centres, ambulances, health visitors, vaccination and maternity and child welfare clinics.

The novel and unique features of the British National Health Service were its universal coverage and the fact that it was free at the point of delivery. And while, as Beveridge had pointed out, it was not really free since it was paid for largely by taxation, 'the free NHS' was regarded by the whole population as a great boon. Indeed, this aspect probably accounts for the fact that the NHS has become the most cherished part of the Welfare State.

The massive need which the NHS met and its initial popularity were both illustrated by the huge overspends of the NHS in its first years. Millions of people now received the medical, dental and optical treatment so long denied them by poverty and restricted access. Under the pressure of financial crisis at the end of the period of Labour government and the demands of military expenditure associated with the Korean War, a new, younger Chancellor, Hugh Gaitskell, required the NHS to meet its share of economies by the introduction of dental and optical charges. Bevan saw this as a major betrayal of the free health service and resigned from the government in 1951.

The date set for the beginning of the combined insurance and health services was 5 July 1948. It has been well remarked that this day was one of the greatest in all of British history. It was the day on which, for the first time in British history, the fear of want, poverty and sickness was removed from the psyche of the British people. R.A. Butler, in his memoirs, argued that there was very little in the Labour government's achievements, since these plans had been agreed during war time by the all party coalition, and from a different political perspective it has become fashionable on the left to decry the achievements of the Labour government as missed opportunities in which the great instruments of privilege (the Church, the aristocracy, public schools, private medicine, private insurance, the 'establishment') were left intact. Neither perspective does justice to what had been achieved. The period is always known as 'the age of austerity' and it is true that rationing, controls, food and material shortages, financial crisis and economic dislocation characterised these years. Yet the Welfare State shines like a beacon, as a tribute to a unique time of social solidarity and collective good will. The Attlee government determined that the state would take unprecedented responsibility for the health and well-being of all its citizens. As the Labour Manifesto of 1950 proclaimed: 'Labour has honoured the pledge in 1945 to make social security the birthright of every citizen. Today destitution has been banished. The best medical care is available to everybody in the land.'

This was not mere rhetoric, and Labour's leading historian (Morgan) has concluded that by 1951 'a plausible updated version of a land fit for heroes had been built on the scarred foundation of an ancient, war ravaged community'.

FIVE

The Welfare State in Modern Britain

For some three decades after its creation in 1948 the Welfare State became a largely non-contentious, fixed element in the social and political landscape of Britain. The 1950s and 1960s were a sort of golden age for the Welfare State. Long after the wartime spirit of fair shares and austerity restraints had been relaxed the British people and British politics became firmly wedded to this Welfare State. It had become, like the wallpaper in a familiar and comfortable room, unnoticed and largely taken for granted. This was the phase of what historians are increasingly calling the classic Welfare State.

There were three broad developments which sustained this incorporation of the Welfare State into the British psyche. The first was that these were years, indeed decades, of full employment. Between the late 1940s and the mid-1970s unemployment averaged below 3 per cent, and the enlarged vision for government action was sustained in a period of full employment which provided the Welfare State with such strong roots.

The second important factor was that the Welfare State perceptibly contributed to social justice and greater equality. Modern economic studies have confirmed the redistributional effects of the Welfare State, and during the second quarter of the twentieth century there was a reduction in income inequality. This occurred during a period when, despite the often publicised failures of the British economy with its stop-go policies, the overall wealth of the British economy grew by an average of 2.8 per cent per annum. The third factor which accounts for the strength and popularity of the Welfare State was that its benefits were not restricted to the poorest citizens. The universalism which characterised the British Welfare State had brought into its compass the middle classes who had a stake in its preservation. The Welfare State served the middle classes well, through such benefits as free health care and free secondary and higher education.

The political consequence was that in these years all the main political parties supported and sustained the Welfare State. Two symbolic resignations established the ground rules for the politics of welfare. Bevan's resignation in 1951 demonstrated that the Welfare State was not sacrosanct and that in times of economic crisis it would bear its share of economies. Seven years later the perhaps even more spectacular resignation of the Conservative Chancellor of the Exchequer, Peter Thornycroft, showed, on the other side of the political fence, that welfare was not a sacrificial lamb and should not be disproportionately savaged. While Labour always made political capital of the fact that it had created the Welfare State, Conservatives shared the welfare consensus. For example, a senior minister in the Heath government of the early 1970s recorded:

> We were strongly committed to the post-war economic and social consensus in which the basic goal of economic policy was full employment. We recognised the need for an improved Welfare State. We believed in a society in which the social services should be expanded.[6]

To reflect all-party middle ground agreement, *The Economist* coined the phrase 'Butskellism', thus allying together the philosophy and policy of Labour's right wing under Hugh Gaitskell and the Conservatives' left wing under R.A. Butler.

It is important not to take this pragmatic consensus as reflecting an agreed ideology. The Conservatives have been well described as reluctant collectivists and their aim was to preserve as much of the free market as possible and use welfare policy as a correction to the faults in the market. Labour approached the Welfare State from an opposite position and saw it as a tool for achieving greater social justice and equality. Changes of government did not always lead to changes in policy and it is often the continuities between governments that are more significant than their differences.

The first years of the Welfare State illustrate this point well. Labour introduced dental and optical charges in 1951 and the Conservatives introduced prescription charges in 1952. The one damaging feature of the National Health Service which threatened its continued survival was the apparently uncontrollable increase in costs. In fact, the Guillebaud Report of 1956 showed that, if anything, the proportion of gross domestic product consumed by the NHS was actually in decline. The increase in service costs was due to inflation and the extra services that were being provided. From time to time charges were increased, and prescription charges were abolished in 1965 and then reimposed in 1968. There were no significant policy changes in the late fifties and sixties and as the official historian of the NHS (Webster) has pointed out, there was a danger of the NHS remaining as a political backwater. Waiting lists and increased costs remained a common feature, for as Labour Minister, Richard Crossman, explained, there would be no limit to the demand for improved health care, as such things as kidney transplants, hip replacements and heart bypass operations became part of public expectation.

In mainstream social security provision there were some issues of principle to resolve. In 1959 earnings-related pensions were introduced, with the option for those in occupational schemes to opt out of the earnings-related element. The earnings-related principle was extended by the Labour government to other insurance benefits in 1966. By this time the actuarial basis of the insurance scheme (so close to Beveridge's heart) had been significantly eroded. It was now a commonplace of policy to increase insurance contributions to meet the financial needs of the scheme rather than to justify the level of benefits. It suited governments of both political colours to retain the fiction of insurance, while insurance contributions had effectively become simply another form of direct taxation, though they continued to provide entitlement to benefit which other forms of taxation did not.

By the mid-1960s one of the guiding principles of the Beveridge concept had been significantly undermined. National Assistance had been viewed as a safety net, the need for which would significantly decline as insurance benefits met the range of social needs. Since, as we have already seen, the benefit levels were never really set at an appropriate subsistence level, it became increasingly common for those already in receipt of a basic insurance benefit, particularly pensioners, to have recourse to National Assistance to supplement their income. There were four times as many people on National Assistance in the mid-1960s as there had been in the late 1940s, the vast majority of them already in receipt of insurance benefit. The National Assistance Board prided itself that it was able to offer an individualised service, with home visits to determine particular need. Yet, for many, particularly older people, this revived memories of the household means test, and in consequence National Assistance became a highly stigmatised form of relief and large numbers of those entitled to claim were refusing to do so. This led to the so-called rediscovery of poverty within the Welfare State, which is perhaps better described as a redefinition of poverty.

It is no coincidence that this should have occurred in the mid-1960s when the age of affluence had most obviously replaced the age of austerity. It had been at the 1959 election that Macmillan had gone to the country with the slogan 'You've never had it so good'. The first generation to grow up under the Welfare State was the first mass generation in British history which had surplus income. Conspicuous consumption altered the expectation of the standard of living in Britain, and the social scientists who discovered poverty in the 1960s found many elderly people and those with large families (even when the head of the household was in work) who were unable to participate in what was becoming the expected norms of society. Poverty was becoming a relative and not an absolute concept.

The Labour government introduced a major policy initiative to deal with this new awareness of poverty. The 1966 Social Security Act renamed National Assistance as Supplementary Benefit. In order to address the issue of stigma, supplementary benefit was deemed to be an entitlement (just as insurance was a contractual entitlement) and the procedures for claiming it were simplified. Finally achieving one of Beveridge's goals, insurance and assistance were combined into a new single Ministry of Social Security. The departmental changes were extended even further in 1968 with the merging of the Social Security with the Health Department to form the DHSS, which survived for twenty years. Benefit levels were increased, as were family allowances two years later. Notwithstanding these increases, the poverty lobby claimed that the poor had got poorer under Labour, and this may have contributed to the Conservative victory in the 1970 election.

The Heath Conservative government of the early 1970s further extended the principle of selectivity through means-tested benefits, with some spectac-ular cuts such as the notorious withdrawal of primary school milk which gave rise to the slogan 'Margaret Thatcher, milk snatcher'. Family Income

Supplement was introduced in order to address the issue of low pay and family size, raising into sharp focus the perennial issue of the balance between benefit levels and wages and the scope of work incentives. The minority Labour government of Wilson and Callaghan in the mid-1970s attempted to rationalise the various social security payments in a three-pronged legislative programme. By the 1975 Social Security Act all benefits became earnings related and invalidity benefits were improved for those under retirement age. The Social Security Pensions Act promised inflation-proof pensions related to earnings (SERPS). The Child Benefit Act abolished child tax allowances and combined all children's benefit into a single payment, including those for single parents and for all children. This ambitious programme, which formed part of the Social Contract with the trade union movement and also included more generous housing benefits, turned out to be the last example of the social democratic impulse which had characterised the Welfare State since 1948. There was already a sea change in the economic and political climate which would bring the Welfare State back into the forefront of British politics.

Of course, the changes in opinion did not come about overnight. On the right, there had always been a minority view that the provision of universal benefits was unnecessary and that the burden of welfare constrained economic initiative and enterprise, which in turn accounted for the poor performance of the British economy. The economic crises of the 1970s, with massive inflation, added weight to this intellectual tendency. Labour faced yet another financial crisis, which seemed to have characterised every Labour government since 1931. In a humiliating policy reverse, the Callaghan government was forced to negotiate an IMF loan, conditional upon a programme of deflationary cuts in expenditure, despite increasing unemployment. In 1976 Labour ministers pronounced that 'the party is over' and Callaghan himself told his party 'we used to think that you could spend your way out of recession . . . I tell you in all candour that option no longer exists'. This marked the end of the all-party commitment to maintaining full employment and many historians see this as the watershed in the history of the Welfare State.

The beneficiary of this changed climate was Margaret Thatcher, who not only won the election of

1979, but also, with a more restrictive view of the Welfare State, was returned to office again in 1983 and 1987. The 1980s were to be characterised by unemployment well over two million, cuts in social expenditure and an apparent rerun of many of the arguments, not only of the 1930s, but even of the 1830s. There were some elements in the Welfare State experience which appeared to justify the change in perception. The growth in means-tested selective benefits and the relationship between the levels of benefits, taxation levels (which even the poor now paid) and low wages produced a confusing mix of financial pressures, which led many people to conclude that they were better off out of work than in work. Structural changes in the British economy led to the creation of waste lands reminiscent of the 1930s. Since two and even three generations had not known regular employment, it appeared that the Welfare State was demoralising the poor just as the old Poor Law had done in the 1830s. Where the Victorians talked of a residuum, the 1980s invented the notion of the underclass, demoralised by welfare and losing initiative and independence in a culture of welfare dependency.

Moreover, it could be even be argued that the Welfare State was part of the problem. For example, there were some who argued that teenage, un-married mothers had chosen pregnancy as a route to housing and welfare benefits, or that large numbers of the workless had chosen unemployment because of its benefit attractions. Using the language of Bentham and Chadwick, they claimed that the Welfare State had loaded the dice in favour of idleness rather than industry. Such an ideological stance produced its echo in the rewriting of history. Thatcherite individualism was given its historical justification in the writings of Correlli Barnett. In two powerfully argued books, as much polemics as history, Barnett purveyed a new historical truth that the new Jeruselem had been a mirage. The Utopia promised by the Welfare State could never be delivered and the effort in seeking to achieve it had fatally damaged the British economy. The Welfare State had become 'a dream turned to a dank reality of segregated, sub-literate, unskilled, unhealthy and institutionalised proletariat hanging on the nipple of state maternalism'. From a quite different perspective radical sociologists were criticising the Welfare State's inability to respond to changes in family and gender relationships, in patterns of work and in social risks. The press exposed scandals where individuals or groups suffered through the actual operation of the Welfare State.

The Conservative social policies of the eighties and nineties were inspired by very different values and political objectives from those in the days of welfare consensus. The explicit aim of the Thatcher government was to roll back the power and role of the state, with such notable examples as the privatisation of utilities and public services, the sale of council houses, and a more regressive tax policy (lowering direct taxes and raising indirect taxes), resulting in a widening of the gap between rich and poor. An early indication of the new government's intent was the 1980 Social Security Act, which broke the link between benefits, including pensions, and the rise in earnings and which abolished earnings-related supplements to social security benefits. In fact, because of increased unemployment, social expenditure continued to grow and in the mid-1980s a major review (The Fowler Review) was conducted which was advertised as a new Beveridge Report.

The review produced four White Papers, all called the *Reform of Social Security*, which lacked any of the vision of Beveridge and were highly technical reports, particularly addressing the relationship between benefits and incentives. Under the 1986 legislation benefits were much restricted and, for example, those aged sixteen to eighteen lost their right to benefit and housing benefit was considerably reduced. Supplementary benefit was replaced by Income Support, and Family Income Supplement was merged into a new benefit called Family Credit. In place of the discretionary benefits available previously, these were merged together into a loans scheme under a Social Fund which reduced exceptional payments by two-thirds. Death and maternity grants were abolished and there was an attempt to streamline and simplify administration. Recent studies suggest that as a result of the Thatcher government's policies, those on supplementary benefit or income support rose by over 60 per cent, while those deemed to be in poverty increased five-fold.

A new broom also swept through the National Health Service. The area health authorities were abolished in 1982 when the government decided to inject a new managerialism into the health service. There was a perception, not without foundation, that public services within the Welfare State were geared to producer rather than consumer interest. The 1989 White Paper, *Working for Patients*, led to the creation of a quasi-market within the health service and a division between purchasers and providers of services. This was introduced under the 1990 National Health Service & Community Care Act which also established fund holding by general practitioners. There was an attempt too to make the medical service more responsive to patient needs, articulated in the 1991 Patients' Charter. The Conservative government also sought to strengthen the labour market by introducing a range of training schemes for youth and adult unemployed and by the creation of Training and Enterprise Councils, which would use the private sector to identify skills shortages and assist the unemployed back into work. The Major government gave notice of the changed climate by changing unemployment benefit to 'Job Seeker's Allowance' in 1993. The Conservatives thus replaced a universalist welfare system with a restricted minimalist provision which relied increasingly on individual and voluntary supplementation.

During the eighteen years of opposition Labour also had to rethink its attitude to the Welfare State. There was surely no political mileage to be found in reverting to the high spending state intervention of previous decades for Labour thinkers targetting the middle ground in politics for a renewal of the Labour mandate. If the Welfare State was still part of the Labour armoury, it was to be a very different Welfare State. Labour set up its own think tank, the so-called Commission on Social Justice, in 1994, whose conclusions indicated the changed direction for New Labour.

> Instead of a Welfare State designed for old risks, old industries and old family structures, there is a need for an intelligent Welfare State. . . . Instead of a safety net to relieve poverty we need a social security system that can help to prevent poverty. Instead of a health service designed primarily to treat illness, we need a health policy whose priority is to promote better health. In other words, the Welfare State must not only look after people when they cannot look after themselves, it must enable them to achieve self improvement and self support. The Welfare State must offer a hand up rather than a hand out.[7]

This was to be an indication of the more functional, instrumental and behaviouralist Welfare State which New Labour wished to create. Labour had in Frank

Field a major expert in social policy, who had himself identified many of the weaknesses of the Welfare State as it had developed. Field had particularly identified the corroding effect of means tested benefits which had positively encouraged fraud. He was painfully aware of the downside effects of the altruistic approach which had characterised much Labour thinking, and he called for a partnership between the individual and the state in a form of social collectivism. He wished to create a stakeholders' Welfare State, where individual self interest would act as an imperative for social welfare improvement. His book concluded:

> Britain's present welfare system has the worst of both worlds: it is broken-backed, yet its costs escalate. In its efforts to support it actually restrains the citizen offering disincentives rather than incentives, and educating people only about the need to exploit the system. . . . [it] proposes a restructuring which brings into central drive position the role of self-interest and self-improvement. Its aim is to help individuals create freer and more fulfilled lives. Fifty years after the efforts of the coalition and post-war Labour governments, it is crucial for Britain to recommence the massive task of welfare reconstruction.[8]

The Labour Green Paper, *A New Contract for Welfare* (1998), bears Field's stamp upon it but Field remained in government only a short time, after a split with Blair.

The New Labour government of Tony Blair which achieved power in 1997 had before it a new agenda for welfare reform, based on a 'Third Way' approach developed by Giddens. Blair wished to maintain the values of the Welfare State by adapting it to new social and economic conditions. As Giddens argued, there were three reasons for reform. First, because welfare provision had become out of line with global social and economic change; second, because some aspects of welfare benefits were unsustainable; and third, because there were perverse incentives and contradictions within the Welfare State.

The Blair programme was 'from welfare to work', offering training, education and work experience in order to achieve a rapid transformation of the labour force from dependency into useful employment. The Blair government had accepted the Conservative idea that individuals should make provision for themselves: the new Stakeholder's Pension would be a supplementary personal pension to counteract the shortcomings of the basic state pension, which had long been deemed inadequate. Labour, like previous Conservative governments, also sought to target excessive expenditure in particular areas, for example, the massive growth in the numbers of people claiming invalidity or disability benefit. New Labour, no less than many Conservatives, now showed an abiding and immutable faith in the virtues of work. The New Deal for the unemployed aimed to get the unemployed into work as quickly as possible and had elements of coercion in the background. The Blair government had been much influenced by American workfare ideas, and a restoration of individualism and enterprise was at the heart of Labour economic and social strategies.

One of the phrases which captured the alleged heartlessness of the Thatcher years was Norman Tebbitt's famous exhortation to the unemployed, 'Get on your bike'. Just as this book goes to press, Gordon Brown has updated the sentiment by a clear injunction to the unemployed that work is available if only they will seek it. He declared, 'We will meet our responsibilities to ensure that there are job opportunities. . . . You must now meet your responsibility – to earn a wage'. The Employment Service and the Benefits Agency are to be merged so that a more concerted attack upon unemployment and welfare fraud may be delivered.

The Welfare State has been many times deemed to be in crisis and even, on occasion, to be dead. It clearly persists in the twenty first century, but no longer reflects the universalism or egalitarianism of the Beveridge proposals. In an ironic way, Britain has protected its people from want, but in doing so more by selective than universal benefits, the British Welfare State has acquired much of the character of the Poor Law which it was created to replace. *The Times* greeted the new millennium by reprinting a famous picture of serried ranks of men eating a meal at Marylebone Workhouse. Its caption was 'Shadow of the workhouse in a new century'. Such comments explain why a knowledge of its origins and history is essential for an understanding of the character and dynamics of the contemporary Welfare State.

Notes

1. Twenty-Second Annual Report of the Poor Law Board (1870), p. 10.
2. S. Webb, *Socialism in England* (1889), pp. 116–17.
3. *Pauperism and Distress* : Circular letter to Boards of Guardians (15 March 1886).
4. *The Times*, 1 July 1940.
5. *Control of Land Use*, Cmd. 6537 (1944).
6. J. Prior, *A Balance of Power* (1986), p. 71.
7. *Report of the Commission on Social Justice* (1994), pp. 223–4.
8. F. Field, *Making Welfare Work* (1995), p. 192.

Further Reading

There is a massive and growing literature on the history of social policy and on the contemporary Welfare State. The key books suggested here all have further bibliographical guidance.

Surveys covering the pre-history of the Welfare State include: D. Fraser, *The Evolution of the British Welfare State* (2nd edn, 1984), P. Thane, *The Foundations of the Welfare State* (2nd edn, 1996), A. Digby, *British Welfare Policy* (1989) and G. Finlayson, *Citizen State and Social Welfare* (1994)

The best introductions to the New Poor Law are: M. E. Rose, *The Relief of Poverty 1845–1914* (2nd edn, 1986), A. Digby, *The Poor Law in 19th Century England & Wales* (1982), D. Englander, *Poverty and Poor Law Reform in 19th Century Britain* (1998) and M.A. Crowther, *The Workhouse System* (1981). A valuable recent addition is: L.H. Lees, *The Solidarities of Strangers* (1998)

The emergence and development of the Social Service state is well discussed in: B.B. Gilbert, *The Origins of National Insurance* (1966), and the same author's *British Social Policy 1914–1939* (1970). Other useful studies are: D. Vincent, *Poor Citizens* (1991), M.A. Crowther, *Social Policy in Britain 1914–1939* (1988), and J. Harris, *Private Lives, Public Spirit* (1993)

There is now an extensive literature on the 1940s. The best study of the war years is: P. Addison, *The Road to 1945* (1975); Jose Harris, *William Beveridge* (2nd edn, 1997) is essential reading. On the postwar Labour government see K.O. Morgan, *Labour in Power 1945–1951* (1984) and his longer study, *The People's Peace* (1992). A lively account is to be found in P. Hennessey, *Never Again* (1993). C. Barnett, in *The Audit of War* (1986) and *The Lost Victory* (1995), offers a polemical right-wing view. Key studies on the development of the Welfare State are: C. Webster, *The National Health Service* (1998) and J. Hills, (ed.) *Beveridge and Social Security* (1994). S. Timmins, *The Five Giants* (1995) is an excellent journalistic account of its recent history, and the whole of postwar social policy is admirably dealt with by R. Lowe, *The Welfare State in Britain since 1945* (2nd edn, 1999).

Useful studies which explain the dialogue between past and present include J. Brown, *The British Welfare State* (1995) and the excellent set of essays in R. M. Page and R. Silburn (eds), *British Social Welfare in the Twentieth Century* (1999).

Economic perspectives on welfare are dealt with in N. Barr, *The Economics of the Welfare State* (1987), and A.B. Atkinson, *Poverty and Social Security* (1989). New Labour ideas are best viewed through Frank Field, *Making Welfare Work* (1995). Contemporary debates are well introduced in A. Deacon (ed.), *Stakeholder Welfare* (1996) and *From Welfare to Work* (1997). See also M. Powell (ed.), *New Labour New Welfare State* and R. Walker (ed.), *Ending Child Poverty* (1999). For the Third Way see A. Giddens, *The Third Way and its Critics* (2000).

Index